Thank You Card
by Shari Carroll

SIZE: 4¼" x 5½"

MATERIALS:

idea-ology Trinkets: Grungeboard Wings, Token, Pin

Ranger: Glossy Accents
   Old Paper Distress Crackle Paint
   Frayed Burlap Distress Ink

Papers (*My Mind's Eye* 29th Street Market,
   Making Memories Journal Circle)

Cardstock (½" x 5½" Brown, 1" x 5½" Aqua)

Hero Arts: (Stamps: 'Thank you',
   Antique Brocade; Clear embossing
   powder, Embossing ink, Kraft Notecard)

5" Ecru ⅜" wide lace, 8" Hemp string

1½" Blue paper flower

Paintbrush, Heat gun, Foam squares

INSTRUCTIONS:

1. Cover Grungeboard wings with Old Paper crackle paint. Let dry and crack.
2. Adhere a flower to the center of the wings.
3. Tie Trinket Pin to the hole in the Muse Token and adhere token over flower.
4. Ink the edges of the journal circle and stamp 'thank you' with Frayed Burlap ink.
5. Mount the winged token to the journal circle.
6. Clear emboss the Antique Brocade image onto notecard.
7. Adhere cardstock strips to card edge. Add lace to cover the seam.
8. Mount the finished journal circle to the card.

True Friends Card
by Shari Carroll

SIZE: 4¼" x 5½"

MATERIALS:

idea-ology Trinkets: Pin, Word Token

Ranger: Frayed Burlap Distress Ink, Cut n' Dry foam

Hero Arts (Stamps: Heart Flourish, 'True Friendship';
   Buttons, Notecard, Soft Sand Shadow Ink)

Papers (2" x 2" Book text,
   My Mind's Eye 29th Street Market 1" x 5⅛")

Cardstock (3" x 5⅛" Cream, ¾" x 5⅛" Brown,
   ¼" x 1¾" Teal)

1¾" x 3" White tag

⅛" wide Teal ribbons (8", 6"), 5⅛" Ecru ⅜" wide lace

Fiskars Scallop punch

Sewing machine

Therm O Web foam squares

INSTRUCTIONS:

1. **Card:** Sew a Zig-zag stitch along 1 edge of the Brown cardstock strip.
2. Glue lace below Zig-zag edge. Wrap ribbon across top of Brown strip, securing the ends on the back. Sew buttons to Brown strip.
3. Ink the edges of the Cream cardstock and Street Market paper strip with Frayed Burlap.
4. Adhere Cream and Street Market papers to notecard. Cover seam with embellished Brown strip.
5. **Tag:** Stamp the Heart Flourish with Soft Sand ink onto tag.
6. Scallop punch the edge of the book text, ink edges.
7. Adhere book text and Teal cardstock strip to tag.
8. Fold paper flower in half and adhere to tag.
9. Tie 8" ribbon through the hole of the token and mount to the tag.
10. Attach Trinket Pin to tag and mount tag to the card.

Cards & Trinke

Flying Heart Card
by Karen Wells

SIZE: 5½" x 5½"
MATERIALS:
idea-ology Trinkets:
> Wings, heart, & crown from
> Grungeboard Elements Swirls
Ranger:
> Adirondack Color Wash: Eggplant, Plum
> Adirondack acrylic paint: Gold Dabber
> Distress inks: Broken China, Fired Brick
> Gold Stickles
> Cut n' Dry sponge
Maya Road Maya Mists Copper Metallic
Papers (4" x 4" old book page, 2½" x 3½"
> cardboard, 2⅞" x 3⅞" Gold mat,
> 3" x 4" Turquoise mat,
> 5" x 5" Burgundy mat,
> 5½" x 11" Mustard cardstock)
The Ultimate! glue • Red liner tape • 3-D Zots

Outline swirls with Gold Stickles. Let dry.

INSTRUCTIONS:
1. Fold Mustard cardstock in half to make card.
2. Use the negative portion of a Grunge Swirl design as a mask over the Burgundy background. Mist with the Copper metallic. Let dry. Adhere to card.
3. Adhere Turquoise and Gold mats to card.
4. Cover cardboard with old book page. Sponge on Distress inks. Let dry. Arrange mask and mist with Color Washes. Adhere to card.
5. Paint wings, heart and crown with Gold Dabber. Let dry.
6. Outline swirls with Gold Stickles. Let dry.
7. Glue wings to back of heart.
8. Adhere heart and crown to card.

'Live' Card
by Karen Wells

SIZE: 5¼" x 6"
MATERIALS:
idea-ology Trinkets:
> Mini Mask Florets
> 'live' Adage Ticket
> 3 Sprocket Gears,
> 2 Metal Corners, Word Key
Ranger:
> Distress inks:
> > Broken China, Vintage Photo
> Plum Adirondack Color Wash
> Cut n' Dry foam
Papers (4½" x 5½" Aqua,
> 4⅜" x 5⅜" Yellow, 4" x 4" White,
> 3¾" x 3¾" Burgundy handmade,
> 5" x 12" Burgundy cardstock)
Ten Seconds Studio 3" mini canvas
Decorative fibers
Copper spiral paper clip
Maya Road Maya Mist Metallics (Copper, Garnet)
The Ultimate! glue • E6000 • Red liner tape

Wrap decorative fibers around the decorated mini canvas and tie a key in place.

INSTRUCTIONS:
1. Fold Burgundy cardstock in half to make card.
2. Adhere Aqua and Yellow mats to card.
3. Sponge mini canvas with Broken China distress ink.
4. Arrange mask on canvas and mist with various colors. Let dry.
5. Wrap decorative fibers around canvas and tie a key in place.
6. Sponge edges of 'live' adage ticket with Vintage Photo distress ink.
7. Adhere ticket, gears, spiral clip and corners to canvas.
8. Glue canvas to card.

Dream Card
by Karen Wells

SIZE: 5½" x 5½"

MATERIALS:

idea-ology Trinkets: Crown from Grungeboard Mixed Minis
    'dream' Adage Ticket, Ornate Plate,
    2 Brass Mini Fasteners, Mini Mask Florets
Ranger: Adirondack Color Wash: Eggplant, Plum
    Broken China Distress Ink, Gold Stickles
    Metallic Gold Dabber, Cut 'n Dry foam
Papers (3½" x 4" White, 3⅞" x 4⅜" Burgundy handmade,
    5½" x 11" Black cardstock)
Canvas Corp. 4" x 4" Canvas
Maya Road Mist Metallics (Copper, Garnet)
The Ultimate! glue • E6000 • Red liner tape

INSTRUCTIONS:

1. Fold Black cardstock in half to make card.
2. Sponge distress ink onto canvas heart randomly.
3. Place heart on White paper. Arrange masks on heart and mist with various colors. Let dry.
4. Adhere Burgundy paper, misted White paper and heart to card.
5. Paint crown with Metallic Gold dabber. Lightly sponge Distress ink onto crown. Apply Gold Stickle dots to crown. Let dry. Adhere to card.
6. Place 'dream' Adage Ticket behind the ornate plate.
7. Attach Fasteners and glue plate to front of heart with E6000.

Cut heart from canvas. Sponge Broken China ink randomly onto heart.

Place heart on White card-stock. Apply masks to heart and spray with inks.

Adore Card
by Karen Wells

SIZE: 5½" x 7¼"

MATERIALS:

idea-ology Trinkets: 4 Mini Pins, Trinket Pin
    Floret Mini Mask, 'adore' Adage Ticket
    Clear Fragments: ¾" x ¾" round, ⅝" x 1½" rectangle
My Mind's Eye papers (7¼" x 11" Dark Brown,
    5" x 6¾" Butterscotch, 4¼" x 5¼" Light Brown,
    3⅞" x 4⅞" Chocolate, 3¾" x 4¾" Aqua)
Canvas Corp. 2½" x 3½" Canvas
Stampington stamps ('Zodiac child', Clear small Flourish)
Tsukineko StazOn Black ink pad
Maya Road Maya Mist Metallics (Copper, Garnet)
Decorative fibers, Burlap cloth
Beige acrylic paint • *The Ultimate!* glue • Red liner tape

INSTRUCTIONS:

1. Fold Dark Brown paper in half to make a card.
2. Center and layer papers and attach to card front.
3. Stamp top and bottom of Butterscotch layer with small Flourish.
4. Adhere burlap to card.
5. Place masks on canvas and mist randomly with colors. Let dry.
6. Wind decorative fibers around canvas and tie a knot. Attach pins in the corners and tape to card.
7. Stamp back of round charm with face of young girl in Black ink. Let dry. Paint over stamp with Beige acrylic paint. Let dry. Tie threads through charm and attach to wrapped fibers with a Pin.
8. Trim and glue 'adore' Ticket to back of a Clear Fragment and glue to canvas.

Keys Card

by Karen Wells

SIZE: 5½" x 5½"
MATERIALS:
idea-ology Trinkets:
    4 keys from Grungeboard Elements Swirls
    'Journey' Word Key, 2 Corners
Ten Seconds Studio:
    Plum metal (3⅝" x 3⅝", 5½" x 5½")
    #5 Paper stump, Decorative wheel tool
    Sanding block, Acrylic plate
Papers (4⅜" x 4⅜" Silver handmade;
    5½" x 11" Black cardstock
    3" x 3" cardboard)
5" Checkered ⅜" wide ribbon
Ranger Silver Stickles
Paper towel or soft cloth
The Ultimate! glue • E6000 • Red liner tape
INSTRUCTIONS:
1. Fold Black cardstock in half to make card.
2. Create border with decorative wheel tool on back of small metal and sand lightly. Tape to Silver handmade paper.
3. Wrap ribbon over both layers and tuck the ends behind the Silver paper. Adhere to card.
4. Lightly glue Grungeboard keys to cardboard.
5. Cover the keys & cardboard with metal (Purple side up) and wrap the metal to the back of the cardboard.
6. Emboss keys with paper stump. Sand and wipe clean. Attach metal corners. Apply Silver Stickle dots to corners. Let dry.
7. Tape the metal key section to bordered metal.
8. Glue the Word Key to front with E6000.

Butterfly Key Card

by Karen Wells

SIZE: 5½" x 5½"
MATERIALS:
idea-ology Trinkets:
    Wings from Grungeboard Mixed Minis
    'heart' word key
Cardstock (5½" x 11" Black,
    5¼" x 5¼" Burgundy)
Ten Seconds Studio:
    5" x 5" Dijon metal, BDAD1a mold
    #5 paper stump, Sanding block
    Acrylic plate
Red craft wire • Brown ribbon
Paper towel or soft cloth
The Ultimate! glue • E6000 • Red liner tape
INSTRUCTIONS:
1. Fold Black cardstock in half to make card.
2. Adhere Burgundy mat to card front.
3. Lightly glue wings to Silver side of Dijon metal, leaving ⅜" space between wings. Let dry. Turn over and emboss wings with paper stump. Place the metal on mold and emboss area around the wings. Sand surface with sanding block. Wipe clean.
4. Wind wire around key and tie ribbon. Adhere to metal with E6000.
5. Tape metal to cardstock.

Working with Metal

Using a mold to create interesting texture on metal is easier than you think...and it's fun to do. The raised effect was produced with a sanding block. Just buff off the color on the raised surfaces and you have a professional look in minutes.

These cards are not the sort that someone will appreciate for a moment and dispose of later in the day. They will become artful additions to home decor or treasured keepsakes preserved in scrapbooks for years to come.

Keep Your Memories Forever

Working with Metal

1. Lightly glue wings to Silver side of metal leaving a ⅜" space between the wings.

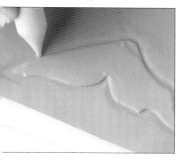

2. Place acrylic plate on a work surface. Position metal with color side up. Emboss with a paper stump.

3. Place metal with color side up over mold with letters facing up. Emboss texture by rubbing with a paper stump.

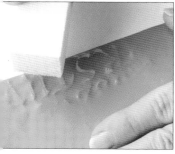

4. With mold still under the metal, sand lightly to reveal Silver color.

Love Always Scrapbook Page
by Karen Wells

SIZE: 12" x 12"

MATERIALS:

idea-ology Trinkets:
  Flourish from Grungeboard Elements Swirl
  'love' Adage Ticket, Ornate plate, 2 Corners
  'memory' Word Key, Swivel Clasp
  Salvage Stickers, 6 Grungeboard Mini Tags

Ranger:
  Eggplant Adirondack Color Wash
  Adirondack Gold Dabber acrylic paint
  Broken China Distress Ink, Cut n' Dry foam

12" Twine, 12" Green 1¼" wide ribbon

K&Company papers 12" x 12" (Green, Brown)

Fiskars circular cutter

The Ultimate! glue, E6000, 3-D Zots

Red liner tape, *Xyron*

INSTRUCTIONS:

1. Mist Grungeboard flourish with Eggplant wash. Let dry. Daub on Gold paint.
2. Sponge Broken China ink onto mini tags. Let dry.
3. Mount salvage sticker letters 'always'.
4. Cut a 3" wide strip of Brown paper.
5. Adhere Brown paper and Green ribbon to page.
6. String twine through tags and mount letters onto the ribbon.
7. Crop and mount photos on page.
8. Add corners to one photo.
9. Glue Grungeboard flourish to page.
10. Glue 'love' adage ticket behind Ornate Plate. Glue plate to page with E6000.
11. Attach key to swivel clasp and attach clasp to twine. Glue key in place with a Zot.

Stone Donut Pendant
by Lisa M. Patterson

SIZE: Pendant: 4"
MATERIALS:
idea-ology Trinkets:
    2 Brass Jump Rings, Foliage metal flowers (two ⅞", one ⅝")
    3¾" Swivel Clasp, 26" Bead Chain with toggle
15mm polymer clay bead
26mm Natural stone donut bead, 2" Copper head pin, Jewelry tools
INSTRUCTIONS:
1. Attach toggle to bead chain.
2. Thread head pin through the hole in the donut bead. Add 2 flowers and the clay bead. Turn the end of the head pin around a jump ring and push the end back into the bottom of the bead.
3. Add the small flower to the jump ring and close the ring.
4. Thread the chain of the Swivel Clasp through the donut bead. Open the jump ring and connect it to the Swivel Clasp. Close the jump ring.
5. Thread the pendant onto the Bead Chain.

Triple Drop Pendant Necklace
by Lisa M. Patterson

SIZE: Pendant: 4½"
MATERIALS:
idea-ology Trinkets:
    26" Bead Chain with toggle clasp, 3" Link chain, 2 Jump rings, 1 Washer
    3¾" Swivel clasp, Foliage metal flowers (one ⅞", two 1", one ⅝")
Ceramic beads with large holes
    (15mm x 21mm, 11mm x 18mm, 11mm x 13mm)
12mm x 15mm Stone bead, 5mm *Swarovski* crystal bead
2 Green vintage glass 7mm beads, 3mm x 12mm glass spacer bead
3 Copper head pins, Jewelry tools
INSTRUCTIONS:
1. Attach toggle to bead chain.
2. String beads, washers and foliage on head pins as desired, ending with a jump ring.
3. Attach pendants to Swivel Clasp with lengths of link chain using jump rings.
4. Thread the ball chain through the Swivel Clasp.

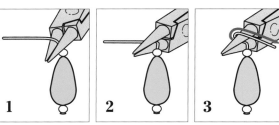

How to Turn a Loop for a Head Pin Dangle

1. Thread a seed bead, drop bead and a seed bead on a head pin. Grasp head pin with round-nose pliers about ⅛" above the bead. Bend at a 90° angle.
2. Loosen your grip on the pliers and pivot them from horizontal to vertical. Apply pressure to the pliers again when your work looks like illustration 2.
3. Wrap the wire over the top jaw of the pliers.
4. Reposition wire on the bottom jaw of the pliers and wrap the wire around it.

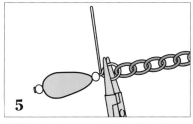
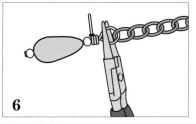

5. Slip the loop on the last link of the 2" piece of chain.
6. Hold the loop in place and begin coiling the wire around the neck. Begin coils as close to the loop as possible. Make 2 - 3 coils, then clip the end of wire close to the coils.

Great Gifts

Slightly eccentric, entirely eclectic, and wholly loved, the extraordinary people in your life deserve unique gifts.

Gift Box
by Carrie Avery

SIZE: 2¼" x 3¾"
MATERIALS:
idea-ology Trinkets:
    Copper Foliage (1" & ⅜" flowers)
    Copper Mini Fastener
    Regal Mini Mask
Candy Tin, Black flat spray paint
Basic Grey Papers
Art Institute Vintage Glass Glitter
Tsukineko Gluepad
Red liner tape
INSTRUCTIONS:
1. Clean and dry a metal tin. Spray the metal box with Black paint. Allow to dry.
2. Cut out paper and adhere to lid.
3. Run Red liner tape around the edge of the lid and cover in glass glitter.
4. Adhere the background of the swirl mask (the negative space) to the lid. Apply glue pad directly onto the open areas of the mask. Press tin firmly into tray with glass glitter. Let dry and gently rub off excess glitter.
5. Assemble foliage with Fastener and adhere to lid.

Crystal Bracelet
by Carrie Avery

SIZE: 6¾"
MATERIALS:
idea-ology Trinkets:
    Link Chain with toggle set
    Clear Fragments (¾" square,
        ⅝" x 1¼", ⅝" x 1½", two ⅝" x 1")
Ranger Glossy Accents
Four 1½" head pins
Crystal beads (4 round 12mm, 2 oval 5mm,
    7 square 6mm, 2 'e')
Wire
Hambly Transparencies
Art Institute Vintage Glass Glitter
Drill
Wire Cutters
Jewelry pliers (Needle-nose, Round-nose)
Red liner tape
INSTRUCTIONS:
1. Cut link chain to desired size and attach toggle clasps.
2. Adhere acrylic fragments to transparency with Glossy Accents. Let dry and cut out with scissors.
3. Drill a small hole in the top of each clear acrylic Fragment.
4. Wrap the edges of the acrylic with Red liner tape. Roll edges in a tray with glass glitter.
5. Attach fragments to bracelet with wire and beads.
6. Attach crystals to bracelet with head pins.

Gear Bracelet
by Lisa M. Patterson

SIZE: 8"
MATERIALS:
idea-ology Trinkets:
    8" Link chain with toggle
    Foliage metal flowers (four ⅝")
    10 Brass Washers
    9 Sprocket Gears
    3 Brass Mini Fasteners
    Jump rings
2" decorative head pins
Vintage shank buttons
Vintage and new glass beads
Jewelry tools
INSTRUCTIONS:
1. Open a few jump rings. Set them aside.
2. Layer Sprocket Gears and affix together with the brads. Add to jump rings.
3. Select 3 - 4 matching head pins. String beads and trinkets. Turn a loop and add a jump ring in each dangle.
4. Attach jump rings to shank style buttons.
5. Continue until you have 20 dangles.
6. Attach toggle clasp to link chain with jump rings.
7. Attach the large gears to the chain first, adding dangles to fill in the space.

Sew Happy Card
by Carol Wingert

SIZE: 5" x 7"
MATERIALS:
idea-ology Trinkets:
    Foliage: Assorted Leaves and Flowers, about 1"
    4 Mini Fasteners (2 Brass, 1 Copper, 1 Nickel)
Cardstock ($4\frac{1}{2}$" x $6\frac{3}{4}$" Black; Ivory: 7" x 10", $4\frac{3}{8}$" x 5",
    $8\frac{1}{2}$" x 11" for computer printing sentiment)
Tan cotton fabric circles (one 4", two 3"), Awl or T-pin
12" narrow Brown ribbon, dotted or stitched, Sewing machine
$4\frac{3}{8}$" x 5" of a tissue sewing pattern, Needle, Thread
Ivory paint, Bristle paintbrush, PVA glue, Glue stick
INSTRUCTIONS:
1. Fold Ivory cardstock in half to make card.
2. Adhere Black mat to card.
3. Crumple the tissue pattern and smooth over the Ivory cardstock, allowing some wrinkles for texture and glue down.
4. Lightly dry brush Ivory paint over the surface of the tissue.
5. Sew a Straight stitch around the 4 sides.
6. Glue the tissue panel to the Black mat.
7. Computer generate the sentiment 'sew happy for you'. Cut out and adhere to card.
8. Fabric Yo-yo's: Fold a $\frac{1}{4}$" hem around the edge of each circle. Sew a Gathering stitch using a single thread with a knot at the end. As you sew, pull the thread to gather the fabric until it begins to turn itself into the center of the circle.
9. When finished, check to make sure the gathers are even and that the part turned into the center is also even. Secure with a double knot.
10. Insert an awl or paper piercer through the center of the yo-yo and insert a metal foliage set.
11. Adhere ribbon stems and yo-yo flowers to the card.
12. Attach metal leaves to the center stem with a Mini Fastener.

1. Sew a $\frac{1}{4}$" hem with a Gather stitch.

2. Pull to draw up the edge.

3. Punch a hole in the center of the yo-yo.

4. Attach flower with a brad.

Steppin' Out Card
by Judy Ross

SIZE: $5\frac{1}{2}$" x 6"
MATERIALS:
idea-ology Trinkets:
    Grungeboard (5" x $5\frac{1}{2}$", $\frac{3}{8}$" x $5\frac{1}{2}$"), 2 Corners, 8 Snaps
Ranger:
    Adirondack Alcohol ink applicator, Worn Lipstick re-inker,
    Distress Inkpads: Black Soot, Worn Lipstick, Vintage Photo
Cardstock (Kraft: 6" x 11", $4\frac{1}{2}$" x 5"; Glossy $3\frac{1}{2}$" x $4\frac{3}{4}$")
Graphic 45 papers (Communique Collection Society Page, On the Dot)
B-Line Designs stamp Fancy Footwork
Ivory lace (5" of 1" wide, 3" of $\frac{1}{4}$" wide), $1\frac{1}{2}$" of Red $\frac{1}{2}$" wide rickrack
Sanding block, Heat gun, *The Ultimate!* glue
INSTRUCTIONS:
1. Fold 6" x 11" Kraft cardstock in half to make a card.
2. Ink edges of card and small Kraft cardstock with Worn Lipstick.
3. Drag the Black Soot pad across both pieces of Grungeboard.
4. Wipe with paper towel and sand.
5. Squeeze re-inker onto applicator and apply to Grungeboard.
6. Dry with heat gun.
7. Adhere small Kraft mat to large Grungeboard. Attach Corner pieces and adhere to card front.
8. Ink the edge of glossy cardstock with the Vintage Photo pad.
9. Stamp image onto glossy cardstock and a scrap of paper to use as a cutting pattern.
10. From scrapbook paper, cut skirts to cover the stamped skirts.
11. Glue lace, rickrack and snaps to skirts.
12. Glue lace to the bottom of the Glossy cardstock and adhere to card.
13. Adhere skirts, strip of Grungeboard and snaps to card.

50 Card
by Carol Wingert

SIZE: 5" x 7¼"
MATERIALS:
idea-ology Trinkets: 2 Numerals
7¼" x 10" Ivory cardstock folded in half
Graphic 45 papers
    (4½" x 6¾" communiqué, One 3-image panel)
3⅝" x 6⅝" Black cardstock mat
2 Black 1¾" scalloped squares
Computer generated sentiment for card
1 yard Red waxed linen, Brown ink, Ink applicator
Glue stick, Needle with large eye
INSTRUCTIONS:
1. Adhere communique paper and Black mat to card.
2. Center a metal number on the Black scallop. Use waxed linen to 'stitch' numbers to the squares.
3. Adhere the 3 image panel to the Black panel and computer generated sentiment to the card.
4. Glue numeral squares on the left/right images.
5. Ink card edges and sentiment with Brown ink.

1. Stitch number to the Black scallop square.

2. Adhere the Black panel to the card.

Sing Card
by Judy Ross

SIZE: 4¼" x 5½"
MATERIALS:
idea-ology Trinkets:
    2⅜" x 4" Swirl Grungeboard
5½" x 8½" Black cardstock
DigitalCollageSheets.com
    ATC Collage collection #6
Tweety Jill papers (4" x 5" text, 2¼" x 4" dotted for mat)
Ranger: Distress ink pads (Broken China, Vintage Photo)
AccuCut
    (die cut machine, bird die)
The Ultimate! glue
INSTRUCTIONS:
1. Fold Black cardstock in half to make a card.
2. Ink the edges of the text paper and glue to card.
3. Die cut bird from Grungeboard.
4. Drag inkpads over the negative portion of the die cut.
5. Adhere dotted paper behind the die cut and adhere to card.
6. Cut out collage images and glue to card.

' ? ' Card
by Carol Wingert

SIZE: 4" x 9¼"
MATERIALS:
idea-ology Trinkets: Stencil type question mark
Cardstock (Black mats: 2¾" x 7¾", 1" x 1¼"; Ivory: 8" x 9¼" folded in half to make a card, ¾" x 1" mat, 2" x 2" to line tin)
2" x 2" metal tin
Computer generated sentiment
Travel rubber stamps, Inks (Black, Brown)
Pop-dots adhesive, Glue stick, PVA glue
INSTRUCTIONS:
1. Stamp travel/postage images with Black ink around the perimeter of the card and on 2" Ivory square to line tin.
2. Distress card, tin liner, and ivory mat with Brown ink.
3. Adhere Ivory square inside the tin.
4. Adhere the stencil to the Ivory mat and small Black mat.
5. Use Pop dots to adhere the stencil panel inside the tin.
6. Computer generate sentiment. Cut out, distress with Brown ink.
7. Glue the Black mat, tin, and cut out words to the card.

1. Stamp travel images on the card.

2. Adhere matted stencil inside tin with a Pop-dot.

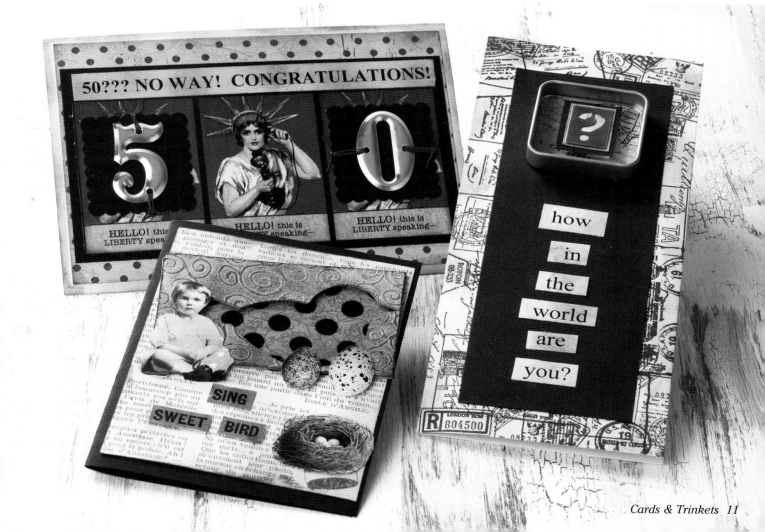

1. Adhere Grungeboard shapes to the front cover.

2. Apply glue over the cover and lay mulberry paper over the board.

3. Squish the wet paper against the Grungeboard with your fingers, conforming it to the shapes.

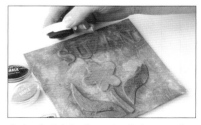

4. Apply ink to the raised shapes of Grungeboard on the cover.

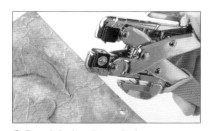

5. Punch holes through the covers and cardstock pages.

6. Bind the book with D-Rings. Attach Trinkets, keys, jump rings and beads.

Mulberry Paper and Flowers Book Cover
by Carrie Avery

SIZE: 6" x 6½"
MATERIALS:
idea-ology Trinkets:
    Grungeboard (Basics, Alphas, Elements)
    3 Book D-Rings, 3 Hinge Clips, 2 Jump Rings
    Swivel Clasp, Trinket Pin, Word Key, Word Tag
    Stencil Type, Sprocket Gears
Papers (Mulberry paper or tissue paper, Cream cardstock)
Assorted beads & charms
ColorBox Chalk ink pads
We R Memory Keepers Crop-A-Dile hole punch
Wire, Wire cutters, Jewelry pliers
The Ultimate! glue, Double-sided tape
INSTRUCTIONS:
1. Cut Grungeboard into 6" x 6" squares for album.
2. Adhere Grungeboard shapes to the front cover.
3. Apply a liberal amount of glue over the entire front cover and lay mulberry paper over the board. Using your fingers, squish the wet paper against the Grungeboard, conforming it to the shape. Let dry.
4. Apply ink pads directly to the surface of the cover starting with the background. Apply ink to the raised Grungeboard part of the cover. Ink cover edges with Brown.
5. Punch holes through the covers and cardstock pages.
6. Bind the book with D-Rings.
7. Attach Hinge Clips to cover.
8. Attach key to bottom D-Ring; Gear & Word Disk to top ring.
9. String charms and beads on wire to create dangles.
10. Attach dangles and Stencil letter to D-Ring with a Swivel Clasp. Attach a Word Tag with a Trinket Pin.

Pieces of Me
Scrapbook Page

by Carrie Avery

SIZE: 12" x 12"
MATERIALS:
idea-ology Trinkets:
    Clear Fragments in sizes to fit photos
Bisous papers
Rub-Ons (7gypsies, Daisy D's)
Ranger Glossy Accents, Double-sided tape
INSTRUCTIONS:
1. Adhere Clear Fragments over photos with Glossy Accents glue. Let dry.
2. Cut out excess paper and photos around the edges.
3. Layer papers on 12" background paper.
4. Tape Clear Fragments to page.
5. Apply rub-on titles and small phrases.

1. Adhere Clear Fragments over photos with Glossy Accents glue.

2. Cut out excess paper and photos around the edges.

Birthday Card

by Carrie Avery

SIZE: $4\frac{1}{4}$" x $4\frac{1}{4}$"
MATERIALS:
idea-ology Trinkets:
    Foliage metal flowers ($\frac{3}{8}$", $\frac{7}{8}$")
    Brass Mini Fastener
AMuse square card
Bisous (3" x 3" Flower paper,
    $3\frac{1}{4}$" x $4\frac{1}{2}$" White cardstock)
4" *May Arts* Ivory $\frac{1}{4}$" wide ribbon
Inkadinkado Happy Birthday stamp
Ranger Walnut Stain Distress Ink
Foam tape, Double-sided tape
INSTRUCTIONS:
1. Attach Foliage to flower paper with a Mini Fastener.
2. Wrap ribbon to back side of paper and tape in place.
3. Tear bottom edge of White cardstock and ink edges.
4. Adhere flower paper to White cardstock mat.
5. Stamp words. Adhere mat to card.

Birthday Angel Card
by Carrie Avery

Make a wish come true by sending someone you love a beautiful card that says, 'I'm thinking of you on your special day.'

SIZE: 5" x 7¾"

MATERIALS:

idea-ology Trinkets:
　　Wings from Grungeboard of Nature Shapes
　　Florets Mini Mask
5" x 7¾" White card
Cardstock (4½" x 7¼" Light Blue, 4¾" x 7" Pink)
Images or photos (Grass, Girl with bunny)
My Tattered Angel Glimmer Mist Spray
ColorBox Chalk ink pads
Foam tape, Double-sided tape, Pop-Dots

INSTRUCTIONS:

1. Adhere Pink mat to card.
2. Apply swirl masks to Light Blue paper and spritz Glimmer Mist. Remove mask while spray is still wet. Continue masking and misting as desired. Tip: Removing the mask while the medium is still wet will give a softer edge. If the mask is left on while the medium dries, the design edge will be crisp. Let dry.
3. Computer print phrase on Blue paper and adhere to card.
4. Apply ink pads directly to grungeboard wings, layering colors as desired. Spritz with Glimmer Mist. Let dry.
5. Cut out images leaving the grass intact. Snip grass along the top edge.
6. Adhere the grass to Blue paper, leaving the girl portion loose.
7. Adhere wings behind the girl's photo with Pop-dots.

Since the invention of paper, books have possessed a magic that transports us to places unknown, introduces us to ourselves, and opens our eyes to the many delights of the universe. This is particularly true of art books. Indulge yourself with a journey of creative discovery and create a book of your own.

1. Cut 24 squares 1½" x 1½" from metals, Grungeboard, fabric, and canvas. Paint, emboss, and embellish as desired.

2. Arrange and adhere to cover. Paint Grungeboard letters and adhere for title.

3. Wrap Trinket Pin with wire and adhere to painted Grungeboard butterfly as a body.

4. Bind book with D-rings. Add ribbons to rings.

Au Naturale Book
by Lisa M. Patterson

SIZE: 5" x 7"

MATERIALS:

idea-ology Trinkets: 5" x 7" Grungebook
Grungepaper, Grungeboard (Nature, Shapes)
2 D-rings, 2 Trinket Pins, 3 Mini Fasteners
Nickel Foliage (5 flowers, 2 leaves)

Ranger: Adirondack Paint Dabbers (Stream,
Pool, Pink Sherbet, Wild Plum, Raspberry,
Sail Boat Blue, Clover, Cloudy Blue, Citrus)
Sticky-Back Canvas, Crackle Accents

Ten Seconds Studio: Metal (Appletini, Chocolate,
Periwinkle, Plum, Kiss Me Pink)
Molds (BDAD1, BDAD2, BDAD3, K1, K2, K3)
Humungo Tape,

2" x 5" of denim fabric, Transparency acetate
Silver wire, Assorted ribbons
Assorted Rub-ons, *Uni-ball* Signo White gel pen
Black fine tip pen, Sanding block, Adhesive
We R Memory Keepers Crop-A-Dile hole punch

INSTRUCTIONS:

Covers:

1. Cut 24 squares $1\frac{1}{2}$" x $1\frac{1}{2}$" from metals,
Grungeboard, fabric, and canvas. Emboss over
the molds (refer to page 5), and embellish as
desired. Arrange and adhere to cover.
2. Paint Grungeboard letters and adhere for title.
3. Wrap Trinket Pin with wire and adhere to
painted Grungeboard butterfly. Adhere to cover.
4. Adhere metal pieces to book.
5. Bind book with D-rings. Add ribbons to rings.

Pages:

1. Paint around the edges of each page and cover.
2. Cut 3 pieces of acetate 5" x 7". Distress with a
sanding block for a frosted look. Apply rub-ons to
both sides. Paint around the edge. Let dry.
Punch holes.
3. Cut 3 pieces of canvas 7" x 10". Fold to be 5"
x 7". Paint canvas and let dry. Punch holes. Add
photos as desired.
4. Crop photos as desired. Position on page without adhering and lightly draw a pencil line around each. Remove images and paint swatches. Mount photos. Doodle around photos with pens.
5. Paint and crackle shapes from Nature Grungeboard. Adhere to pages.

Pages left & right - Mark photo placement. Paint a frame on the page.

Page right- Apply a rub-on to sanded acetate.

Page right - Emboss Green metal for the flower leaves.

Pages left & right - Doodle around photos with gel pens.

Page right - Wrap a small butterfly with wire. Shape the antennae.

Page right- Apply a rub-on to sanded acetate.

Life Album
by Carrie Avery

SIZE: 5" x 6¾"
MATERIALS:
idea-ology Trinkets:
    3 circles from Grungeboard Shapes
    3 small Game Spinners, Stencil Type letters, Mini Pins
    Long Fasteners
Cosmo Cricket papers
7 gypsies Book kit, Waxed Linen, *Lineco* Bookbinding Needle
Eyelets, Eyelet Tools, *Marvy Uchida* 1" hole punch, PVA glue
INSTRUCTIONS:
1. Cover the spine and covers with paper.
2. Add eyelets to the holes in the spine.
3. Punch holes in pages and bind following the book kit manu-
facturer's instructions.
4. Attach mini pins to the spine. Adhere stencil letters to cover.
5. Punch 1" paper circles and adhere to grungeboard circles.
6. Punch a hole through the middle of each circle. Attach a
spinner and a word disk to each circle using a Long Fastener.
Adhere each circle to the book.

Secret Story Binder Cover
by Karen Wells

SIZE: 5" x 7"
MATERIALS:
idea-ology Trinkets: 1 Keyhole & 2 Bookbinders from
    Grungeboard Elements Swirls, 'Story' Adage Ticket
    Ornate plate, Word Key, Swivel clasp, 10 Brass Mini
    Fasteners, 2 Copper brads, Timeworks Mask,
    Regal Mini Mask
Ranger: Distress Inks (Broken China, Marmalade)
    Adirondack Eggplant Color Wash
    Cut n' Dry foam, Copper Stickles
Maya Road: 5"x7" binder book
    Maya Metallic Mists (Garnet, Copper)
3" x 7" Canvas cloth
Limited Edition Text stamps,
Tsukineko Brown StazOn ink
The Ultimate! Glue • E6000 • Red liner tape

INSTRUCTIONS:
1. Sponge Distress inks
onto binder.
2. Randomly stamp text
images with Brown ink.
3. Arrange masks on cover
and spritz alternately with
Color Wash and mists.
Arrange swirl mask on canvas and mist. Let dry.
4. Sponge Broken China ink
onto the Grungeboard
pieces. Let dry.
5. Tape canvas piece to
book binding.
6. Attach Mini Fasteners to
Grungeboard pieces and
glue to book.
7. Glue 'story' ticket to
back of ornate plate, attach
with brads. Connect key to
swivel clasp and attach to
ornate plate. Adhere plate
to book with E6000.
8. Dot Copper Stickles
along the edge of the
canvas binding.

1. Score Grungepaper every ½" on a Scor-it Board.

2. Ink and stamp as desired.

Calendar
by Judi Kauffman

SIZE: 5" x 9¼"

MATERIALS:

idea-ology Trinkets:
Grungepaper (3½" x 4½" for title, 2¼" x 3½" for calendar mat, for images: 1⅛" x 2¾", 1" x 2½", ⅝" x 2⅜")
Grungeboard (5" x 8" background, 4" x 5" title mat)
Ranger Nick Bantock inks
(Chrome Yellow, Prussian Blue, Vermillion Lacquer)
HAMMONDSgroup Scor-it Board
1½" x 3" calendar pad, Assorted wooden beads
Stanislaus Imports triangle brads (Antique Bronze, Green)
Wire, 3 round craft sponges
Red Castle, Inc. Rango Zoo rubber stamps
Sakura of America assorted Gelly Roll Moonlight pens
Label maker with Blue tape
Beacon ZipDry paper glue

INSTRUCTIONS:

1. **Title:** Place the 3½" x 4½" Grungepaper (textured side down) on the Scor-it Board. Use the scoring tool to create raised ridges at ½" intervals parallel to the long side. Turn paper and repeat to create ridges parallel to the short side. Flip the Grungepaper over to see the de-bossed 'grout' lines.
2. Sponge Yellow ink onto the tiles, followed by Vermillion and a bit of Blue. Drag the edges in Blue. Randomly stamp spiral swirl in Blue.
3. **Calendar mat:** De-boss two lines parallel to the long edge of Grungepaper. Sponge and stamp as above.
4. **Background:** Sponge as above; drag the edges in Blue.
5. **Title mat:** Sponge Vermillion onto the edges of board.
6. Stamp small animals onto Grunge scraps. Trim so that the stamped strips will fit between the tiles' grout lines. Accent stamped images with Gelly Roll pens.
7. Print words with label tape. Cut out letters in a square.
8. **Assembly:** Glue layers together as in photo. Add letters, calendar pad, and triangle brads. Attach a beaded wire as a hanger.

Earth Day Card
by Judi Kauffman

SIZE: 6" x 6"

MATERIALS:

idea-ology Trinkets:
Grungepaper (5½" x 5½", 2¾" x 2¾", ⅝" x 2⅜" for title)
Ranger: Big & Juicy Rainbow ink pad (Foliage, Hydrangea)
Cardstock (2" x 3" Ivory for title mat, 6" x 12" Burgundy for card)
HAMMONDSgroup Scor-it Board
24" Olive Green ³⁄₁₆" wide raffia
Stanislaus Imports 3 Dragonfly brads, 4 Copper brads
3½" x 3½" Clear acetate or vinyl, Ecru waxed linen
Rubber stamps (*Lisa Pavelka* Tooled Leather,
EK Success Small Alphabet)
Chenille needle, Round craft sponge, Craft knife, Cutting mat
Beacon (Kids Choice Glue, ZipDry Paper Glue)
Foam squares or dots, Pressed leaves

INSTRUCTIONS:

1. Lay Grungepaper square on Scor-it Board with textured side facing up. Use scoring tool to emboss parallel lines 1" and 1¼" from each edge of the square.
2. Using light hand pressure, sponge color from the Orange end of the Foliage pad onto the square to highlight the embossed lines.
3. Stamp Tooled Leather onto 2¾" Grungepaper square using Brown. Stamp Tooled leather onto Ivory cardstock scrap using Blue-Purple. Sponge and smudge color with Orange onto this scrap. Stamp words onto Grungepaper title piece. Tear a strip of stamped Ivory cardstock to fit below the rectangle.
4. Cut slits on both sides of embossed ridges. Weave raffia along sides of the square.
5. Use waxed linen to sew an 'X' over raffia in the corners of the square.
6. Add dragonfly brads angled along raffia.
7. Glue stamped square and message block in place. Glue leaves to center square. Attach acetate covering the leaves with a Copper Fastener at each corner.
8. Place Burgundy cardstock face down on Scor-it Board, score and fold in half.
9. Adhere embellished Grungepaper square to card using foam squares.

1. Drag ink pads across the Grungeboard shapes.

2. Mist lightly with water to make the colors bleed. Dry with a heat gun to stop the color bleeding.

3. Mist with Glimmer Mist inks.

4. Stamp with StazOn ink.

Journey Card
by Judy Ross

SIZE: 5" x 7"
MATERIALS:
idea-ology Trinkets:
   Grungeboard
      4⅞" x 6¾"
   Crown from
      Grungeboard
   Mixed Minis
   4 Sprocket Gears
   1 Ornate Plate
   2 Mini Fasteners
Ranger
   Mini-Mister
7" x 10" Yellow card-
stock folded in half
Rubber Stamps:
Stamper's Anonymous
   Tim Holtz Fairytale
   Frenzy
Delta Rubber Stampede
   Woman in Repose
Postmodern Design
   Tape measure
Inkadinkado Script
Marvy Uchida ink pads
   Yellow Green,
   Yellow, Rose Marie
   Caribbean Blue,
Tsukineko StazOn
   Black ink
Tattered Angels Glimmer
   Mists (Golden Terra
   Cotta, Iridescent
   Gold, Lemon Zest)
Heat gun
The Ultimate! glue
INSTRUCTIONS:
1. Apply inks directly to Grungeboard and the crown.
2. Mist lightly with water, allowing the inks to bleed. Dry with a heat gun.
3. Spray with Glimmer Mists and dry with a heat gun.
4. Stamp with StazOn ink.
5. Glue Sprockets and crown to Grungeboard.
6. Attach plate over 'Journey' word with Mini Fasteners.
7. Adhere Grungeboard to front of card.

Karen Wells
Karen's art is widely published and sold in galleries. She designs cards and projects for rubber stamp companies, die-cutting and Ten Seconds Studio. View more in the gallery of www.tensecondsstudio.com.

Judy Ross
Judy has appeared on HGTV and DIY showcasing mixed media talents. As an owner of The **Creative Quest** paper arts store, she keeps current with all the new trends. Teaching classes across the US is her passion.

Shari Carroll
Known for her collage art, this active artist creates technique articles, cards, blogs, catalog samples and designs. She enjoys traveling and teaching stamping classes worldwide.

Carrie Avery
Carrie's favorite creations include soldered glass charms, hand made books and albums, photography, and mixed media collage. Her work can be viewed at www.paperwingsproductions.com.

Lisa M. Patterson
Lisa is a wonderful mixed media artist and TENseconds Studio certified designer. You may view more of her original work and creativity on her blog at www.lisapatterson.typepad.com

Judi Kauffman
Judi is a nationally known designer, writer, teacher, and product developer. Her expertise includes scrapbooks, rubber stamps, paper crafts, collage, knitting, needlepoint, crochet, weaving and fabric art.

Carol Wingert
Carol runs an online project kit business called "creatologie from carol wingert studio", with monthly kits. To see samples of her art, check out her blog at www.carolwingert.typepad.com.

MANY THANKS to my staff for their cheerful help and wonderful ideas!
Kathy Mason • Kristy Krouse
Patty Williams • Donna Kinsey
David & Donna Thomason